The FLUMPS

1 Sometimes, after tea, Grandfather told the young Flumps stories of long ago, when Flumps were brave and very fierce.

2 "In the olden days," began Grandfather, "there lived a Flump called Captain Pike." The children listened very closely.

3 The story ended with him saying, "The last I heard of old Captain Pike, he had sailed right over the edge of the world!"

4 Later the young Flumps went for a walk. "I don't believe Grandfather's sea story," said Perkin. "It sounds a bit fishy to me."

5 Suddenly, Perkin fell. He saw himself falling over the edge of the world. "Help!" he cried. "I believe the old story now!" he said.

6 "You only tripped over a root," giggled Pootle. "Oh," said Perkin. "You really fell for that one," Posey said, smiling.

Henry's Cat and friends

1 Douglas Dog was building a snowman. "Will you help me finish it?" he asked Henry's Cat. "It's meant to look like you."

2 "Sorry," said Henry's Cat. "I'm going skiing. It's much more fun. Watch me and I'll show you how good I am," he boasted.

3 But Henry's Cat had never been skiing. He was soon in trouble. "Oh, dear me," he moaned, as he sped off down the hill.

4 The hill was too steep and Henry's Cat did not know how to stop. "Look out!" he shouted. It was too late. "Oooh!" he cried.

5 Splat! Henry's Cat plunged into his friend's snowman. "Oh, no!" cried Douglas Dog. "You've ruined my snowman!"

6 "What a splendid snowman," said Mosey Mouse. "It looks just like Henry's Cat. He will be pleased when he sees it!"

1 It had been snowing hard. "Do you think you'll be able to drive in this?" asked Mrs Goggins, when Pat went in to collect the mail.

2 "I'm wearing my boots in case I have to walk," Pat replied. He set off on his round. "My, oh my, the snow *is* deep," he said.

3 It got deeper and deeper. Pat stopped. "This is where I walk," he said. He left his van at the side of the road and set off.

4 When he reached Greendale Farm, Mrs Pottage came out to meet him. "Did you see the milk tanker anywhere?" she said.

5 "No," said Pat. "It must be stuck in the snow." "What are we going to do with all our milk?" said Mrs Pottage.

6 Peter Fogg had just finished milking the cows. "If the tanker doesn't come we'll have to throw the milk away," he said.

7 "Oh, dear," said Pat. "I'll give you a lift back to your van on my tractor," Peter said. "We might meet the tanker."

8 Peter drove the tractor slowly. Its snow plough cut through the drifts. "I could do with a snow plough on my van," said Pat.

9 When they reached Pat's van, there was the milk tanker. "Hello there," called the driver. "I'm stuck. Can you help me?"

10 Peter cleared the snow so that Pat could move his van out of the tanker's way. "Follow me," Peter told the driver.

11 The milk tanker set off behind Peter's tractor. "They won't have to throw out all that good milk now," Pat said to Jess.

1 Gran and Jim had gone to spend a day by the sea. The weather was not warm enough for swimming, but it was sunny.

2 "Let's go beachcombing," said Gran. "Okay," said Jim. They clambered over the rocks picking up shells and pebbles.

3 "Look at this one!" said Jim, showing Gran a big stone he had found. "I've never seen one this shape before. It's really great!"

4 They were so busy collecting things to take home, they did not notice the tide coming in all around them. "Come on," said Gran.

5 "We're cut off!" cried Jim. "No, we're not," said Gran. She started picking up huge rocks to throw into the water. Splosh!

6 She threw enough rocks to use as stepping stones. "Off you go, Jim!" she said. Gran followed until they were safely on the shore.

A letter to Watson

Mr Baskerville entered a competition he saw on a label of Watson's dog food. He won first prize, a week on a sea-cruise for one, so he had to leave Watson behind with Mr Jupiter. Watson did not mind, because Mr Baskerville wrote to him every day. This is one of his letters.

1 "Can you think of anything that is prettier than my dress?" asked Delilah. "Yes," said Morph. "Show me, then," said Delilah.

2 Morph metamorphed into a beautiful, multi-coloured parrot. "It really is pretty," said Delilah. "And it's so bright!"

3 The parrot swooped into the garden. Gillespie was showing Grandmorph his flowers. "Pretty Polly!" it squawked.

4 "My hair looks pretty," thought Folly, as she combed it in front of the mirror. Suddenly, the parrot brushed her aside.

5 "Pretty Polly!" squawked the parrot, as it admired itself in the mirror. But the amazing magic was quickly wearing off.

6 The parrot became Morph again. "Morph isn't as pretty as my dress!" Delilah said. "Or my flowers!" chuckled Gillespie.

Spotty Jo

Jo lay back against her pillows. She was hot and sticky and covered in spots. Her mum came up with a cold drink and sat on the bed. "My head hurts," complained Jo. "I know," said mum. "My spots itch," moaned Jo. "I know," said mum. "Let's think of something for you to do. You could read a book." "It makes my head hurt more," said Jo. "You could draw a picture," said mum. "No," said Jo. "It makes my spots itch more. Tell me about when I was a baby instead." "I'll do better than that," said mum. "I'll show you."

She went away and came back with a big book. She laid it on the bed. "I don't want to read," wailed Jo. "It makes my head hurt." "This isn't an ordinary book," said mum. "It's a photograph album. Inside are lots of pictures of you when you were a baby." "Are they really me?" asked Jo. "Why did you take so many photographs?" "We took them to remember you by," said mum. "Then you'd better take one of me with spots," said Jo. "A good idea," said mum. "I'll go and get the camera." She went away and came back with the camera. She took a photograph of spotty Jo lying in bed. "Now you can remember me with measles," said Jo. "How could I forget?" laughed her mum.

story by Val Willis
picture by Terry Burton

1 "We have a big order of footballs to make by tonight," announced Mr Duncan, one Friday afternoon.

2 "Bertha will have to work hard to make them all by tonight," said Ted. "Well, get cracking then," said Mr Duncan.

3 Panjit brought a case full of leather, while Roy rushed off for the stitching. "It's up to Bertha now," said Ted, pulling the lever.

4 "Whirr," went Bertha. They all waited for the first ball to appear. "Are you playing football tomorrow?" Ted asked Roy.

5 "Not sure yet," answered Roy. "One of the players is sick." "You could play for them, Ted," said Flo. "You used to be good."

6 "That was years ago," laughed Ted. "Will you play for us?" asked Roy. "I'd like to. But I'm a bit out of practice," said Ted.

7 Just then, Bertha sent out the first football. It was not at the usual speed, though. It was very fast and she fired it out head high.

8 "Mind out, Nell!" cried Ted, leaping at the ball. He caught it and passed it to Flo. "That was a good save!" shouted Roy.

9 Then Bertha shot out another ball, then another. Ted was diving everywhere. Nell and Flo quickly packed them into boxes.

10 Soon, the whole factory was watching and clapping, as Ted caught the balls. They were now shooting out even faster.

11 "Good old Bertha. The order will be ready tonight," said Mr Willmake. "And I'll be ready to play tomorrow!" puffed Ted.

Spot the difference

There are eight things missing from the second picture. Can you spot them?

HEADS and TAILS

wasp beetle

carpet beetle

Colorado beetle

musk beetle

The wasp beetle gets its name because it looks a bit like a wasp. It has a long body and antennae. The carpet beetle lives indoors and eats furs and sometimes blankets. It has two spots on its back.

The Colorado beetle is from North America. It has a flat striped body. It eats crops especially potatoes and should be caught and taken to a police station if found. The musk beetle is bright green and gives off a musky smell. It lives near willow trees by streams and rivers.

Pigeon Street

1 One spring, Rose and Daisy go out and buy window-boxes. They fill them with soil and plant some seeds. They wonder whose will sprout first.

4 There are no signs of Rose's flowers yet. Every day, Daisy pulls up her flowers to make them look a little taller, as if they are growing.

5 "I wonder why my flowers are taking so long to grow?" thinks Rose. One day, Daisy looks out and sees it is blowing a gale.

2 The next day, Daisy passes a flower shop. She sees some plastic flowers for sale and that gives her an idea. She goes in and buys them.

3 When she gets home, she puts the plastic flowers in her window-box. Rose is very surprised to see that Daisy's flowers have grown so fast.

6 When the wind dies down, Daisy sees that her plastic flowers have blown all over the place. A few have landed next door at Rose's!

7 When Rose sees the plastic flowers in her window-box, she is delighted. "They're so easy to keep," she says. "I can have flowers all year round!"

Buttons throughout

In **January** Gran and Jim go sledging.

In **February** Paddington receives a Valentine.

In **May** Hamlet does the spring-cleaning.

In **June** Bertha makes beach-balls.

In **September** Molly and Polly go to school.

In **October** King Rollo plays in the autumn leaves.

the year

In **March** Henry's Cat goes ballooning.

In **April** Grandmorph eats an Easter egg.

In **July** the Play School toys go to the park.

In **August** the Flumps go to the beach.

In **November** the Magician gives a firework display.

In **December** Postman Pat delivers Christmas cards.

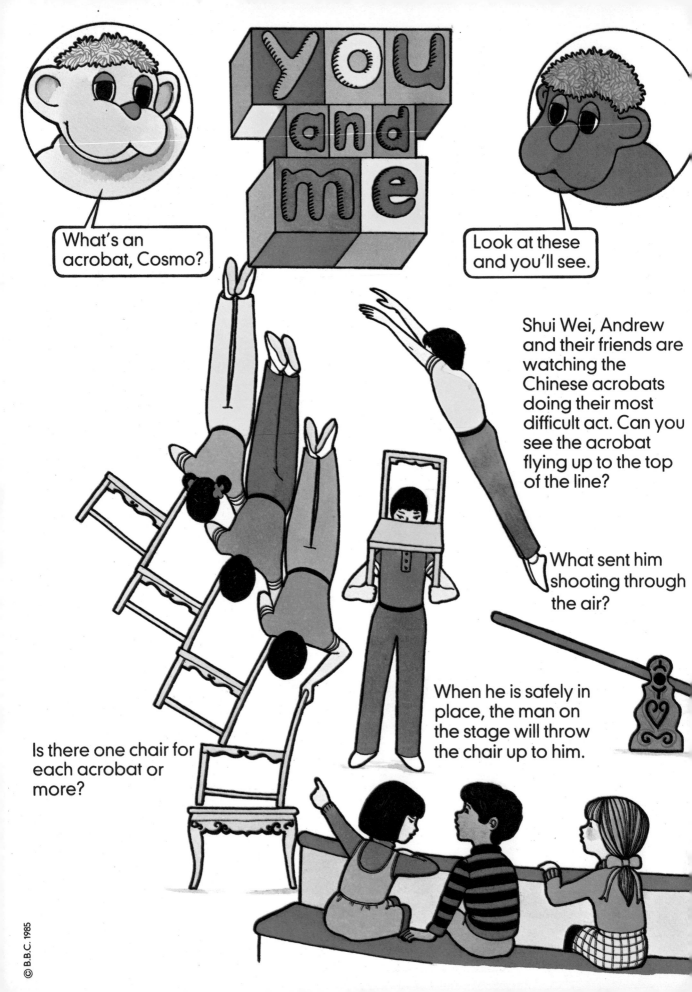

The FLUMPS

1 "Come on, Perkin and Pootle!" cried Posey. "Let's all play football." She grabbed the ball and ran outside.

2 "This looks like a good spot," said Posey. "What can we use as a goal?" "How about these old stones?" said Pootle.

3 Posey was the goal-keeper first. Perkin took a shot, but it missed. "That's odd," he said. "The goal looks smaller."

4 Next it was Perkin's turn in goal. Posey tackled Pootle and took a shot, but it looked like it was going wide.

© David Yates Ltd. 1985

5 Suddenly, the ball was heading for the goal and Perkin could not save it. "Now the goal looks wider," he said, puzzled.

6 "No wonder the goal keeps changing its size," said Posey. "The goal-post is a toad and he looks hopping mad!"

KING ROLLO and the hat

1 King Rollo had been sitting in the sun. "My crown is making me too hot," King Rollo said to Cook. "I'll buy myself a hat."

2 So he went to the beach shop to buy one. The first hat he tried on was far too big. "I can hardly see," he said, giggling.

3 "What about this one, sir?" said the assistant. But it was too small and a bit itchy. "No, sorry," said King Rollo.

4 He went outside again into the sun. "It's still too hot to wear my crown," he mumbled. "I'll try an umbrella. That will do the trick."

5 But the umbrella kept poking everyone. "Put it down," said the Magician. "I'm trying to sunbathe. It's making shadows."

6 "Put a hanky on your head," suggested Cook. But as soon as he did, the sun went in. "I'm all right now," said King Rollo.

The very greedy king

There was once a very greedy king. "I want six cream cakes and an apple dumpling," he would roar. And his cooks would rush around making and baking whatever the king ordered. "Bring me fish and chips and ice-cream and chocolate sauce!" he cried. "I'll have tomato soup and scrambled eggs and trifle and chocolate biscuits!" He was a *very* greedy king. And his cooks were *very* tired out. One day, the king called his cooks to him. "I want you to make me an extra special sponge cake," he said. "I want it to be so light, it

can float." The cooks hurried to the kitchen, looking very worried indeed. A sponge cake so light it could float! They had never made that before.

All night long, they rubbed and mixed and whipped and baked, until eventually, they were satisfied. They put the cake in the oven.

The next day, they carried the sponge cake in to the king. It was so light, they had to hold it down, in case it floated away. The king was delighted. "Wonderful!" he exclaimed as he bit into it. "It's as

light as air." And, being a very greedy king, he ate the whole lot, without giving a piece to anyone. "That was delicious! he sighed, wiping the crumbs from his mouth. Then, something very extraordinary happened. The king began to float off his chair, higher and higher into the air. He floated out the door and up into the sky. Soon, he was only a distant spot on the horizon. And that was the last the cooks ever saw of the greedy king.

story by Ann Burnett
pictures by Chris Duggan

1 One day, Pat received a present from his cousin Bill in London. "It's a barbecue!" Pat said, looking pleased. "Let's try it out."

2 Pat went to Mrs Goggins' shop. "Have you any charcoal?" he asked. "And some sausages? We're having a barbecue."

3 "What fun," said Mrs Goggins, handing him the bag. "Come and join us," said Pat. "Food always tastes much better outside."

4 Pat met Ted Glen and the Pottage twins. "Come to our barbecue," he said. Then he met Miss Hubbard and invited her, too.

5 Pat set up the new barbecue and put in the charcoal. "Don't you come too close," he said to Julian. "It will be very hot."

© Woodland Animations Ltd. 1985

6 The charcoal was hard to light and Pat used up a lot of matches. But at last it started to burn. "Hooray!" he cried.

7 By this time, all the guests were arriving. "Hello, Pat," said Ted. "I've brought along my barbecue tongs to hold the sausages."

8 "We made you a hat," said Katy. "It's a chef's hat," said Tom. "Thank you," said Pat. " Isn't it smart?" The twins giggled.

9 Soon, the barbecue was glowing brightly. "Now we're ready to cook the sausages," said Pat. "I'm looking forward to this."

10 But just then, the rain began. Big drops fell on the coals and made them sizzle. It rained so hard that it put out the fire.

11 Pat had to cook the sausages on the stove. "They taste just as nice this way," said Mrs Goggins. Everyone agreed.

Snowman game

Use a different coloured pencil for each player.
Take turns to draw a line between any two dots.
As soon as a square is made, draw a snowman
inside. The player with the most snowmen wins!

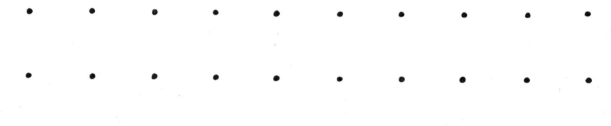

Play School jigsaw

Trace the picture on to paper and colour it in. Then stick it on to card and cut out the pieces. Jumble them up and try to put the jigsaw together.

1 An overnight storm had blown down a wall at Spottiswood's. And, inside the factory, there were more problems.

2 Mr Sprott was designing a new game of snakes and ladders for Bertha to make. "Bother!" he said. "I'm all in a muddle."

3 "Your plans look very big," said Tracy. "I hope Bertha understands them." "So do I," said Mr Sprott, giving them to Ted.

4 Ted fed all the information into Bertha's computer. Then he filled her with paint and cardboard and pulled the start lever.

5 Bertha did not seem too happy. "Bang! Clonk! Bang!" she went. Ted peered inside. Suddenly, he jumped back in surprise.

6 A huge dice rolled out and chased Ted around the factory. Everyone laughed. Luckily, Tom managed to stop the dice.

7 Everyone crowded around. Mrs Tupp had just shouted, "Tea up!" when a massive snake's head appeared.

8 "Oh, dear," sighed Mr Sprott. "I wrote down the wrong sizes. The game is far too big and Bertha's making it in sections!"

9 "Never mind," said Tracy. "I have an idea." When Bertha had finished making the huge game, they carried the pieces outside.

10 "We'll mend the wall with it," said Tracy. They stuck the pieces to the wall. "It's the brightest factory ever!" said Mr Willmake.

11 "Let's use the dice to have our lunch on," said Roy. "Good idea!" cried the others. "Back to work!" shouted Mr Duncan.

1 Tony was away and there was no heating on in the studio. "Perhaps it will be warmer under-the-table," thought Morph.

2 But it was no warmer down there. "I am going to write a letter of complaint to Tony," said Delilah, very crossly.

3 Morph read over Delilah's shoulder as she scribbled. "Dear Tony," she wrote. "How naughty of you to leave the heating off!"

4 "Give this to Tony!" ordered Delilah when she had finished writing. "It's not a very nice letter," thought Morph. "Poor Tony!"

5 When Delilah was not looking, Morph metamorphed into a letter-box. "That's a good idea. I'll post it!" said Delilah.

6 But the letter did not drop as Delilah had expected. Instead, the letter-box started to eat it. "Chomp, chomp," it went.

7 "Stop!" shouted Delilah. But it was too late. The box enjoyed the letter and was now looking for more paper to eat.

8 Grandmorph was sitting quietly, reading his newspaper. The letter-box snatched it from his hands and gobbled it up.

9 Gillespie and Folly were putting up paper chains for Christmas. The letter-box saw them and started to eat them all.

10 With every scrap of paper gone, the letter-box became Morph again. He made a leap for the table top.

11 When Tony returned, Morph told him about the complaints under-the-table. The heating was turned on again.

12 Then Tony made decorations. "Hooray for Tony!" they all cried. The under-the-table home was ready for Christmas.

Join up the dots then colour in the picture.

HEADS and TAILS

stonechat

whinchat

wheatear

redstart

These birds belong to the thrush family. The stonechat is seen over moors, heaths and cliffs around Britain. The male has black, white and chestnut feathers, while the female has lighter coloured feathers. The whinchat is a summer visitor to Britain. The male has a white eye strip and dark brown and orange feathers.

The wheatear nests in holes in the ground. It arrives in late March for summer. Both male and female have white and grey tail feathers. The redstart is colourful and is found in woods, heaths and parkland.

The ballet lesson

Maggie liked to play in the garden. She liked making mud-pies and looking for worms. Maggie liked getting dirty. She did not want to learn to dance. She did not want to wear ballet shoes that had to be kept clean and were hard to tie up. Maggie liked her wellies. Sarah, who lived next door, went to ballet lessons. "I'm going to be a fairy in the ballet show," she told Maggie, as she danced around her. "Mind my worms, you nearly stood on them!" Maggie shouted.

"Maggie," called her mum. "Would you like to go to ballet lessons with Sarah?" "No," said Maggie. "You'll enjoy it," said her mum. "I won't. I don't want to go and I don't want to wear ballet shoes. I like my wellies," said Maggie. In the end, Maggie said she would go, on one condition, she could wear her wellies. Sarah laughed. "Nobody wears wellies for dancing!" she said. "I do!" said Maggie.

When they got to the hall, Maggie stamped inside. The other girls were putting on their ballet shoes. They giggled when they saw Maggie. Maggie glared at them. Then, the ballet teacher came in. "I need one of you to be a giant in the show," she said. "Who wants to be a giant and stamp about in a pair of wellies?"

Maggie stepped forward. Perhaps ballet lessons were not such a bad idea after all!

story by Sue Habberley
picture by Chris Duggan

The FLUMPS

1 "I think it's going to rain," Mother said, when the Flumps were out walking. "It won't rain today," said Grandfather.

2 Suddenly, it started to pour. "Quick, run for it!" cried Father. "We can shelter under that tree over there. Come on!"

3 Luckily, the tree was big and there was enough room for all of them underneath. "I hope it stops soon," sighed Pootle.

4 But it kept on raining heavily. "Now it's dripping through the leaves on to our heads!" cried Posey. "I'm soaking!"

5 "Well, come on, everyone," said Father. "We'll just have to make a run for it back home." Perkin dashed off first.

6 Then he stopped. "Look!" he said. "It has stopped raining and we've been standing under the tree getting wet! Aren't we silly?"

1 Henry's Cat was thinking about his name. "I wonder who Henry was?" he thought. He decided to ask Constable Bulldog.

2 "Do you know why I'm called Henry's Cat?" asked Henry's Cat. Constable Bulldog looked rather puzzled.

3 "Well, er . . ," he began. "I'm not sure, but perhaps, long ago, one of your family lived with a famous man called Henry."

4 Henry's Cat was so excited, he rushed to tell Chris Rabbit. "We should find out more," he said. "Let's go to the library."

5 Chris Rabbit found a book called Kings and Queens. He read about kings called Henry, but not one cat was mentioned.

6 Henry's Cat read a small book called Famous Cats, but he did not find a famous *Henry's Cat*. "Still, I can dream," he sighed.

Gran

1 One day, the postman came with a letter for Gran. "I hope it's not a bill," she said. "I've had far too many bills lately."

2 It was not a bill, but an invitation to a fancy dress party. "What fun!" said Gran. "Now, what can I go as? Something unusual."

3 Jim had received an invitation to the same party. "What can I go as?" he said. "I must think of something really unusual."

4 He went to see Gran to talk about it. They thought it would be fun to go as pirates. "I can just see us," said Jim. "Can't you?"

5 "But there will be lots of pirates. Let's go as something different." They looked at each other and then started to smile.

6 They both had the same idea. Jim dressed up as Gran and Gran dressed up as Jim. "Most unusual!" said Gran, laughing.

KING ROLLO and the balloons

1 King Rollo had been asked to start the hot air balloon rally in the village. "What's a hot air balloon?" he asked Cook.

2 "It's a huge balloon that's filled with hot air," she said. "It's attached to a basket and people can fly away in it."

3 "It doesn't sound very safe," said King Rollo. The next day, he went down to the village. The balloons were very colourful.

4 Some people were still blowing up their balloons, but soon they were ready. "And they're off!" shouted King Rollo.

5 They did look lovely as they flew off into the sky. "I'd like to go up in one," said King Rollo. "But I might not like it."

6 Later, when he arrived home, King Rollo had an idea. "It's safer than the others," he told Cook. "At least I won't take off!"

Help King Rollo find his way through the clouds to land safely on the grassy hilltop.

1 Molly and Polly have asked Reg if they can play with some sand they have found on the Green. It is sand for a sand-pit and easy to model.

© B.B.C. 1985

4 Mr Jupiter comes along and sees the statue. He thinks it really is Mr Baskerville. "Good morning," he says. Mr Baskerville does not reply.

5 Mr Jupiter goes on talking. Then he wonders why Mr Baskerville is so silent. Flash wonders, too and goes up to the statue and sniffs it.

2 They run home for their buckets and spades then start to make something. "Let's make someone from Pigeon Street," says Molly.

3 "How about Bob and Reg?" says Polly. "I know, Mr Baskerville!" They make a sand statue like Mr Baskerville saying, "Hello!"

6 The more Flash sniffs at it, the more suspicious he becomes. Finally, he barks and jumps up at the statue. Mr Baskerville crumbles into a heap.

7 Mr Jupiter is very surprised to see his friend disappear. Molly explains it was a statue. "Wasn't Flash clever for noticing?" says Mr Jupiter.

Jamie's Father Christmas

The week before Christmas must be the longest week of the year, the days seem to pass so slowly. Jamie thought Christmas Eve would never come. To make matters worse, Grandad had been strangely absent. Every morning, he left the house at 8.30 and did not return until the evening. It was all very mysterious and Jamie tried to imagine what Grandad could be doing that took up so much time. Grandad teased him, saying he was training for the next Olympics. Jamie's mum just said it was secret, top secret!

When Christmas Eve came at last, Jamie was so excited that he did not know what to do with himself. He stood at the window, gazing at the grey garden and hoping for snow. Mum was making sausage rolls and mince pies. "Why don't you help me?" she asked. Jamie tried to help, but he could not concentrate. He put sausage meat in the fruit mince pies and fruit mince in the sausage rolls. "Come on, put your coat on," said mum, when they had finished. "Let's go into town to see the Christmas lights."

When they arrived, it was getting dark. Jamie hardly recognised the High Street. It was hung with lots of coloured lights and crowded with shoppers. Mum led the way to the biggest department store and there, in the entrance, Jamie saw the figure of Father Christmas. He was ringing a bell as he collected money for the old folks Christmas dinner. Mum gave Jamie some money and he pushed it into the collecting tin. Then, Father Christmas winked and said, "Thank you, Jamie." Jamie looked puzzled. "Grandad? Is that you?" "Sssh!" whispered Grandad. "Don't tell everyone." "Isn't it time you finished for today?" said mum. "It certainly is," said Grandad. "I'll just get changed." "Oh, Grandad!" said Jamie. "Couldn't you come home like that?" "Well . . . I suppose so," said Grandad, chuckling. "It is Christmas Eve after all."

So Jamie walked home hand in hand with his very own Father Christmas. Grandad waved to all the children they passed and Jamie thought it was the best Christmas Eve he had ever had.

story by John Firman
pictures by Colin and Moira Maclean

Christmas decorations

Paper lanterns:
Fold an oblong of paper in half. Cut from the folded edge as shown. Open out the paper and bend to form a lantern. Tape the edges. Make a paper handle and hang it up.

Hanging spirals:
Place a plate on paper and draw around it. Draw a spiral on the circle and cut it out. Sew cotton through the centre and hang it up.

Christmas peppermints

You need:
1 egg white
peppermint essence
9oz icing sugar
food colouring

Whisk the egg white until it is frothy.

Add icing sugar and stir until mixture is stiff.

Add a couple of drops of peppermint essence.

Add food colouring.

Roll out mixture and cut into shapes. Place on waxed paper.
Leave for a few hours in a warm, dry place.

Postman Pat

To Postman Pat
Greendale
LA21 8ZX

1 "Could you check the bell ropes for me, Pat?" asked the Reverend Timms. "One seems to be frayed at the top. It might break."

2 Pat climbed up into the belfry to look at the ropes. "They seem all right," he said. Then, he heard a strange little noise.

3 "Cheep! Cheep!" "Whatever's that?" said Pat. He looked around and there among the beams was a nest of baby birds.

4 "Well, I never," said Pat. "What a funny place to build a nest." The mother bird was perched nearby with some worms.

5 "I'll leave you in peace," said Pat, climbing down the ladder. "Is everything all right up there?" asked the Reverend Timms.

6 "Yes and no," Pat said. "The ropes are fine, but I'm afraid we won't be able to ring the bells for several weeks."

7 "A blackbird has built her nest up there." "Bless me," said the Reverend Timms. "What are we going to do for bells?"

8 "People won't know when it's time for church without bells," said Pat, thoughtfully. "I wonder what we can use instead?"

9 Pat drove off on his round. When he was passing the school, he suddenly stopped. "A-ha!" he said. "That's what I need."

10 On Sunday morning, Pat went to the church. But instead of going in to ring the bells, he stood outside the front door.

11 DING! DONG! DING! DONG! Pat was ringing the school bell! "I think we'll do sums today," joked the Reverend Timms.

Paddington has broken
three biscuits. Can you
fit them together again?

Henry's Cat and friends

1 It was very cold and Henry's Cat and his friends had to stay inside. "I wish it was summer," moaned Mosey Mouse.

2 "So do I," said Henry's Cat. "Then we could all go to the seaside for the day. There's nothing like sunbathing!"

3 "Who needs sunshine when we have our warm fire?" said Chris Rabbit. "We all need some sunshine," said Henry's Cat.

4 "And I have a brilliant idea!" he cried. "All it takes is a few pots of paint and we *will* be at the seaside. Watch this!"

5 Henry's Cat painted a picture of the seaside on the wall. Then he put on his sunglasses and sat in a deck-chair.

6 "This is fun!" shouted the others. "It sure is," said Henry's Cat. "And this beach is right beside the kitchen and all the food!"

How many Happy Buttons can you find?

Learn the Green Cross Code with Buttons

1. Find a safe place to cross, then stop.

2. Stand on the pavement near the kerb.

3. Look all around for traffic and listen.

4. If traffic is coming, let it pass.

5. Look all around again.

6. When there is no traffic, walk straight across the road.

7. Keep looking and listening for traffic while you cross the road.

Stop! Look! Listen!

1 "Whatever are you doing, Tracy?" asked Mr Sprott. "There's a mouse under here," she replied. "It ran over my foot and under the table."

2 Mr Sprott looked under the table, too. The mouse ran straight past him, out of the door and down the stairs, to the workshop.

3 "I'll follow it," said Tracy. "Will you show Ted my designs for the lion pyjama-cases at the same time?" asked Mr Sprott.

4 When Tracy reached the workshop, the mouse was nowhere to be seen. She gave the designs to Ted. "Thank you," he said.

5 Ted fed Bertha with the instructions and pulled the start lever. "Off you go, Bertha," he said. "Whirr, buzz, whirr," she went.

6 Then, Roy heard a squeaking noise. It was coming from inside Bertha. "What's wrong, Bertha?" asked Ted. "Are you feeling ill?"

7 "Shall I send Tom inside to see what's wrong?" asked Roy. "Good idea," said Ted. Roy placed Tom on the delivery belt.

8 As Tom went inside, the squeak stopped. "Bertha is cured!" said Roy. Suddenly, the little mouse ran out from inside Bertha.

9 It was followed by Tom who had one of the lion pyjama-cases over his head. Bertha gently lifted Tom down to the ground.

10 Tom chased the mouse right out of the factory. "The poor mouse must think Tom is a giant cat!" said Ted, laughing.

11 Tracy saw the mouse go and Ted told her what had happened. "Well done, Tom," she said. "Good old Bertha!"

KING ROLLO and the snowman

1 It was snowing heavily outside. "Yippee!" cried King Rollo. "I can make a snowman." "You wrap up well first," said Cook.

2 So King Rollo put on his coat and went outside. He picked up handfuls of snow. "I can't grab enough!" he moaned.

3 "It will take me ages," he muttered. The Magician had been watching him from the castle. "I'll help you," he shouted.

4 "Make a ball and roll it in the snow," said the Magician. So King Rollo did that and together they rolled the snowball.

King Rollo © David McKee 1985

5 It grew bigger and bigger and BIGGER! Soon, it was bigger than them. "There," said the Magician, putting in the eyes.

6 "What an unusual snowman," said Cook. "And it's huge!" Everyone in the village came to look. King Rollo was pleased.

The Teds marshmallow clusters

Ask someone to make these for you.

You need:
1oz butter
2oz cornflakes
12 marshmallows

Melt the butter
and marshmallows.

Remove from heat
and add cornflakes.

Spoon mixture into
paper cases.

Leave to cool and then eat!

© B.B.C. 1985

The FLUMPS

1 "It's nasty weather outside," thought Pootle. "Just the right sort of day to stay indoors and do a painting."

2 Pootle decided to paint Mother, who was busy in the kitchen. "You will have to paint me as I'm walking about," she said.

3 Every time Pootle was about to start, Mother left and all that was left on the paper was a smudge and a blur.

4 "Sorry, can't stop," said Mother, as she hurried past. Pootle did his best to keep up. The paint splashed everywhere.

5 "Finished!" he cried. He showed Mother his painting. "I painted the things on the table because they stood still," he said.

6 "It's very good," said Mother. "And now it's about time I sat still for a while." Pootle poured her a nice big cool drink.

1 Jim was spending the afternoon by the river. It was a warm, sunny day and Jim enjoyed just sitting and looking.

2 The water flowed by him quite quickly, carrying with it old twigs and leaves. Sometimes, a fish would make ripples.

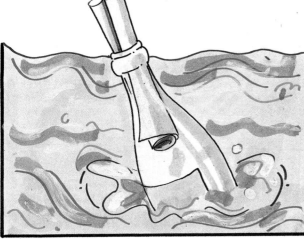

3 Then suddenly, Jim saw a bottle with a piece of paper inside, floating past. "A message in a bottle!" cried Jim.

4 He went down to the water's edge and managed to fish the bottle out of the water. He took the paper out to read.

5 "This is a message from Gran," he read. "I've been watching you from the other bank. Turn around and you will see me!"

6 Jim turned around and there was Gran smiling at him. "I bet you thought it was a secret message!" she said, laughing.

Play the Buttons board game:

You need a dice and a different coloured button for each player.

Throw the dice to see how many squares to move. The winner is the first one to reach the finish.

START

Miss a turn.

Uphill slope.
Miss a turn.

FINISH